Teaching Writing with the Microcomputer

by
E. Marilyn Schaeffer

Library of Congress Catalog Card Number 86-63877
ISBN 0-87367-254-2
Copyright © 1987 by the Phi Delta Kappa Educational Foundation
Bloomington, Indiana

This fastback is sponsored by the Miami University Chapter of Phi Delta Kappa, which made a generous contribution toward publication costs.

The chapter sponsors this fastback to celebrate its 20th anniversary and to honor its past presidents.

Table of Contents

Some Problems in Teaching Writing

Since the early 1970s researchers have been investigating the way writing is taught in American schools (Britton et al. 1975; Emig 1971). They found that most teachers are concerned with the final product of writing — the story, the essay, the report — but have little understanding of the process that successful writers use in creating the final product. Traditionally students have been asked to produce compositions on demand, with little guidance on how to work through the steps that quality writing requires.

By analyzing how student and adult writers compose, researchers have developed effective strategies for teaching students to write (Collins and Sommers 1985). Called the process approach to teaching writing, this method has received widespread endorsement from both researchers and educators. Proponents of this method regard writing as an ongoing, multi-stage process, with equal emphasis given to each of the stages. These stages include prewriting (organization), composition, revision, and post-writing (presentation of the paper to an audience).

Those who advocate the process approach believe that to communicate effectively, the student writer must first do research to gather information and to organize that information before composition is begun. Then a first draft is written, after which the student critically evaluates the composition as a whole to determine whether the sequencing, the content, the format, and the tone communicate the intended message.

Whether writing is taught through the process approach or more traditional methods, one of the roadblocks to producing good writers in the elementary school is that students have to use pencil and paper as the only means of transcription. Younger students have difficulty with handwriting and labor painfully over the first draft. To them, making revisions and recopying becomes an overwhelming burden. It is heartbreaking to see a young student tear up and throw away a well-written composition because repeated erasures have made holes in the paper.

Even older students who have mastered handwriting skills end up wasting time and energy in copying and recopying a composition. The original enthusiasm the student had for the writing assignment may evaporate in frustration and anger, causing the student to approach the next assignment with anxiety and apprehension. Students may refuse to try out new ideas if extensive reorganization requires hours of drudgery in recopying. Some student (and adult) writers make only those changes that do not require recopying, regardless of how much revision would improve their compositions.

Because of the problems mentioned above, many teachers report that students are less than enthusiastic about writing. It is my belief that many teachers would demand more editing and revision if recopying were not so time-consuming and tedious for students. Fortunately, this problem can be solved through the word-processing functions of the microcomputer.

Solving Writing Problems
with the Word Processor

The microcomputer is a marvelous tool for elementary school students, who should practice writing skills daily. It can virtually eliminate the problems attendant to transcribing compositions with pencil and paper. Its word-processing functions allow the writer quickly and easily to type over what has previously been typed, to insert new text within the old, to crase sections as large or small as desired, and to print a final copy that is both legible and professional looking.

The components of a microcomputer are a monitor or screen, a keyboard, a one- or two-disk drive (a two-disk drive is preferable), a connected printer, and the software package with the instructions to the computer for carrying out the word-processing commands. Depending on the brand purchased, the cost for the whole unit usually runs between $1,000 and $2,000. School systems often can obtain significant discounts from manufacturers and software vendors, especially if several computers or software packages are purchased at once.

There are many different word-processing packages on the market today, with an increasing number designed specifically for elementary students. Each of these software packages is different, with different capabilities, different commands for carrying out the various functions, and varying levels of difficulty for users. Despite these differences, there are some functions that appear in virtually all word-processing software: 1) the writer can instantaneously view on the monitor what is being typed on the keyboard; 2) it is possible to edit the typed document both before and after it has been printed; 3) it provides long-term storage of documents on tape or a floppy disk; and 4) documents can be reproduced on a printer when it is hooked to the computer.

Proofreading and editing are easy with a word processor. Even a beginner can use the delete, strikeover, and insert functions to make simple changes. Students can make corrections in grammar, spelling, or vocabulary quickly and easily with no need for recopying. They can make more complex changes with only a brief period of practice, such as changing the order of the sections of the paper or adding passages written in another draft.

Teachers testify to the enthusiasm with which students approach any activity on the computer. Using the word processor for writing tasks capitalizes on that enthusiasm, thus heightening motivation for writing. Teachers report that students who use word processors for the various stages of writing have an improved attitude toward writing in general, tend to make more revisions, write longer papers, and pay more attention to detail (Smith 1985).

The literature reports mixed findings as to whether students who use word processors do more complex revision than those who do not use them. Some studies have found that students make the same sorts of mechanical errors and do about the same level of revision with a computer as they do when writing longhand (Hult 1985; Kurth and Stromberg 1984; Wheeler 1985). Others have found that students tend to produce higher quality compositions and their revisions tend to be more complex when writing is done on the word processor (Fischer and Fischer 1985; Hunter 1984; Mercer, Correa, and Sowell 1985).

After careful examination of these studies and others, it is my view that the difference in findings may be due more to the method used to teach writing (for example, the emphasis that teachers in the studies placed on revision) than to whether or not the students used word processors.

Regardless of the mixed findings, it seems obvious that those students who have access to a word processor would find the sheer volume of work involved in transcribing and making revisions less than would those who have to revise and recopy by hand. While the word processor is no panacea for the struggling writer, when properly used it can be effective in easing the struggle (Hunter 1984).

If students go through the steps advocated in the process approach to writing, their sense of accomplishment in their work should grow. When their compositions communicate the desired message to the intended audience, students can rightly take pride in their writing. When they run out the final copy on the computer printer, it has a professional look. In fact, even rough drafts look good. This can be helpful in the proofing and editing process because it is easier to make corrections on legible copy. And multiple copies can be run quickly when the teacher wants to make student compositions available to audiences outside the classroom.

Throughout each stage of the writing process, the word processor can free the writer from restraints that inhibit the free flow of words and ideas. Students are free to take risks in their writing because they can always change their minds. The writing potential of students can come nearer to realization if administrators and teachers recognize the contribution that word processors can make to the act of writing (Phenix and Hannan 1984).

The Word Processor as a Writing Tool in the Elementary Grades

Several states have mandated or soon will mandate that students be computer literate by the time they graduate from high school. Some states will include assessment of computer skills on statewide achievement tests. Most of these states have designed an instructional sequence for teaching computer skills K through 12. The targeted skills almost always include mastering word-processing techniques.

As with any area of the curriculum, the developmental level of students will determine when to teach the various components of word processing. Although most of the commands are fairly simple to master, some cognitive skills are required, such as remembering and following a sequence of instructions. The sequence of commands taught should be closely integrated with the writing curriculum for the various grades. For example, it would be inappropriate to try to teach the commands to move whole paragraphs to a first-grader who is capable of putting together only a few sentences to tell a simple story.

In the following sections I shall examine children's developmental levels as they relate to the writing curriculum for the elementary grades and suggest a sequence for teaching word-processing skills. Also, I shall describe general computer skills that should be taught at each grade level in order to put the teaching of word-processing skills in context. This skills progression is derived from the *Florida Computer Literacy Scope and Sequence,* which identifies the skills to be introduced, reviewed, and assessed at each grade level.

The skills progression presented here assumes the sequence begins in kindergarten. At this time not many schools start computer training this early. However, even if word processing is not introduced until the intermediate grades, students can move through the same progression of skills, but more quickly, until they reach the desired level of competency. With increasing emphasis on computer education in many states, the time cannot be too far off when all students will have access to computer equipment and training.

Kindergarten: The Process Begins

Developmentally most kindergartners live in an egocentric world in which play is indistinguishable from work. Because of their limited cognitive abilities, they cannot yet generalize broad concepts and rules from their experiences. Their language arts exercises should deal with subjects familiar to them in the here and now. They are learning to write their names and a few other words related to their recent experiences (Rogers 1982).

Kindergartners are introduced to the alphabet and learn to recognize the shapes and sounds of letters. They also learn that words are formed by blending the sounds of a sequence of letters. Decoding and encoding words is begun using both phonetic analysis and word recognition by configuration. Increasingly, kindergartners are learning to read and write simple sentences.

First, kindergartners should be introduced to the various components of the computer and their functions. These include the keyboard, monitor, disk drive, and printer. The teacher then demonstrates that by putting a diskette into the disk drive, something appears on the monitor; and by striking keys on the keyboard or using joysticks or paddles, the monitor changes. Kindergartners should also understand that something typed on the keyboard can be run out on the printer.

Since kindergartners are learning to recognize and name letters, the logical place to begin with the word processor is to teach them to recognize and use the letters on the keyboard. In computer terminology, typing is called keyboarding. There are software packages on the market specifically designed to teach young children keyboarding skills. One of the best is Scholastic's *ComputerGarden*, which was developed with kindergartners and first-graders in mind. This package includes a teacher's manual with detailed lesson plans, a 4' x 8' durable plastic keyboard that is placed on the floor for gross motor activities, student workbooks, and computer software providing students structured practice with the letters on the keyboard.

Using *ComputerGarden*, the children begin with gross motor activities on the brightly colored keyboard on the floor. These activities are tied together with a fanciful continuing story. In one lesson the children learn that their fingers must hop like bunnies across the keyboard. The suggested activity is to have them physically hop across that row of keys on the keyboard on the floor. Another lesson has

Kindergartners enjoy learning about the computer keyboard by playing games on a large plastic keyboard on the floor.

them crawl across the bottom row of letter keys since the fingers must "dig down" like worms to strike those keys. After completing the gross motor activities, the children move on to fine motor activities where they begin to learn the correct finger positions for using the letter keys. Kindergarten and first-grade teachers give this package high marks because of its bright colors, the high-interest continuing story, and the carefully planned sequence of student activities. They describe the package as truly "user friendly."

By using *ComputerGarden* or a similar package, kindergartners can learn basic keyboarding skills needed for word processing. This is probably sufficient for kindergarten level because until the children can readily locate and use letters on the keyboard, they are not ready for even the simplest word-processor software. However, teachers can demonstrate how a word processor works by entering and printing stories dictated by the children.

First Grade: Introducing a Simple Word-Processing Package

The cognitive world of six-year-olds is more organized. With more accumulated knowledge, they are beginning to understand their environment. While their thinking is becoming more complex, they still are unable to think logically about their experience. Social interaction is limited mostly to immediate gratification of needs (Rogers 1982).

First-graders can be taught how to care for diskettes, how to turn the computer on and off, and how to use the computer safely. One first-grade teacher issues a computer "license" when her students have learned how to use computer equipment. She presents the licenses with solemn ceremony, explaining that they are just like a license to drive a car; that is, students must pass a test before they are issued the license, must show the license whenever they use the computer equipment, and may have their license revoked if they break the rules. The teacher reports that only one of her students has had a license revoked; and when he saw other students working at the computer when he could not, he worked very hard to have his license reinstated. This type of licensing system could be adapted for use at any grade level or with any computer skill.

Handwriting for first-graders is manual labor in both senses of the term. In writing a story, they must painstakingly copy each letter, which makes it difficult for them to concentrate on their flow of ideas. For this reason, teachers have never expected six-year-olds to produce compositions of any length; but by using a word processor, we are finding that young children's writing is surpassing our wildest expectations. An excellent example is provided in the following excerpt from a first-grader's composition about using the *Pet Story Writer* word-processing package (Phenix and Hannan 1984).

BY TIMMY

THE PET ES GD FOR CEDS THET DOT NOW HOW TO SPEL THER IS A MENUW UUY CAN ERAS UOYR STORE UOY CAN PRENT UOYR STOREY UOY PRES RUN STOP TO GET THE MENU THE PET SES HE! MY NAME IS STOREY RITR WOTS UOYRS . . .

Timmy's whole composition ran 21 lines, quite a lengthy "story" for a six-year-old. His paragraph is perfectly understandable despite his inventive spelling and lack of punctuation.

With first-graders, teachers should continue to develop their keyboarding skills. On mastery of keyboarding, students can be introduced to a simple word-processing package such as *Bank Street Writer* or *Story Writer*. At this level teachers should concentrate mainly on teaching students to record their stories rather than on correction of spelling and grammatical errors, which requires the use of editing commands.

As with most skills taught in first grade, teaching word processing requires that the teacher demonstrate the skills several times and supervise students closely while they practice them. The teacher should have the computer set up for the students before they sit down to write. Learning how to open and close a word-processing system will be taught at a higher grade level. The important thing here is for first-grade students to record their stories.

Students are thrilled to see a story that they have written run out on a computer printer. Seeing their stories perfectly typed is a great motivation for them to write on their own. A teacher who runs a computer lab where small groups of children are scheduled for 30 minutes a week reported that one group of first-graders wrote extra stories in class during the week so they could see them in print when they came to the computer lab.

A large-type print wheel is recommended for kindergarten and first grade because large type is easier to read. If a large-type print wheel is not available, teachers can decrease the number of characters printed per inch on the printer. Although the size of the letters does not change, increasing the spacing between letters makes the text easier to read.

Children enjoy illustrating their stories after they are printed. Their drawings also can inspire them to write additional stories. One word of caution: Do not put paper with crayon or paint on it through a printer because particles may drop off and damage the equipment.

First-graders are not intimidated by computers; they quickly learn how to use a simple word-processing system. If time and care are taken to ensure that they have mastered the skills at first-grade level, the foundation will be set for them to use the microcomputer as a writing tool throughout their school years.

Second Grade: Simple Revision Commands

Second-graders are beginning to use elementary forms of logic and reasoning and are able to describe a sequence of events. This higher level of cognitive development is reflected in their writing. They can now link several sentences together in sequence to tell a story that goes beyond describing what is happening to them personally. They are still somewhat egocentric but are now capable of understanding that viewpoints of others may not always coincide with their own. Their writing assignments should still be centered on their own personal experiences, but can now include descriptions of someone who is going through a similar experience (Rogers 1982).

General instruction at second grade continues to focus on the parts of the computer and their functions. Teachers can demonstrate to individuals or small groups how to turn on the computer, put in a disk, and run a simple program that does not use a menu or prompts, which require reading ability that may be beyond the students' level. With continuing emphasis on the care and handling of hardware and software, by the end of second grade students should be able to use the equipment independently.

Rainbow Keyboarding is an effective software package for second- and third-graders that extends and enhances keyboarding skills begun with *ComputerGarden*. The package includes a teacher's manual, student workbooks, a large keyboard poster for the bulletin board with color-coded keys indicating correct finger positions, stickers to put on the students' fingers to remind them which finger presses which letters, and software for keyboard practice with words of gradually increasing length. Teachers who have used this package say that it is a valuable motivational aid for teaching students letter recognition and beginning writing skills.

Second-graders should learn that the software that contains the instructions for running their word-processing system is called the *program disk* and that what they type is stored on another disk called the *data disk*. They should be aware that the instructions stored on the program disk remain the same each time they use the system, but that the information they enter on the data disk can be changed at later writing sessions.

Some of the simpler word-processing systems like *Bank Street Writer* require the user to switch back and forth between the *write mode* (where the story is typed) and the *edit mode* (where revisions can be made). This may be somewhat confusing at first, but the teacher can explain that the write mode is like using the pencil to write, and the edit mode is like using their eraser to make changes. A simple poster can be made to illustrate this point to students.

Second-graders should learn that some word-processing commands can be entered into the computer through the *control key*, which is held down while a letter key is pressed (much like holding down the shift key to make capitals). Most commands are easy for students to learn since the letter key used is the first letter of the command word, such as CONTROL-D for delete or CONTROL-P for print. Other commands are given by highlighting command words printed at the top of the screen.

Students plan their story before working on the word processor.

Newer computer models use special *function keys* that allow the user to give a command by pressing only one key specifically designated for that command. A common special function key is the DELETE key. When the student wants to "erase" what has been typed, the cursor is placed on the letter to be erased and the DELETE key is pressed. The computer immediately erases the letter from the monitor. Another function to be taught is *strikeover*. To perform this function, the user places the cursor on the letter to be changed and strikes the letter key to replace it.

Most second-graders should be able to type stories and do minor revisions with some teacher supervision. Also, they can work together in small groups to make up a story. Working in round-robin fashion, one student dictates a sentence, a second enters it on the computer, and a third reads it back. Then the students switch roles. In this way each has an opportunity to work at the keyboard, and all are responsible for adding sequential sentences to the story as well as for reading the unfolding story. While the story is being developed and entered on the computer, the students should not be too concerned about spelling or mechanics. Once the story is completed, the students can work together to make any necessary corrections or revisions before their story is printed.

Third Grade: Beginning to Control the System

Third-graders continue to improve in logical thinking to the point where they are capable of categorizing the same objects on more than one dimension. While still operating cognitively at a concrete level, they have begun to interact socially to a greater extent, although friendships may be short-lived (Rogers 1982).

In terms of overall computer skills, third-graders should be able to explain the function of all of the parts of the computer and understand that a computer needs instructions to run. They should be aware that a program is a logical, sequential set of instructions and that different programs are required to make the computer do different things. The teacher can use examples of familiar activities, such as listing the steps for making a peanut butter-and-jelly sandwich or for putting on their shoes and socks, to get across the idea that many tasks require a specific sequence of steps for successful completion.

Third-graders are capable of writing short essays of two to three paragraphs or more in length. They are able to get outside themselves and write about people they know or characters they have read about or seen on television. After composing their stories on the computer and running them out on the printer, they enjoy illustrating them and can put several of them together to form a small book for others to read. When students know that their story books will be read by others, they are motivated to make corrections and revisions so that the final product looks professional. Some schools place bound copies of students' story books in the library for general circulation. Having one's book in the library is a source of pride for the writer and may serve as an inspiration for the reader to compose a book of stories for circulation.

By the end of third grade students should be able to put the program disk and the data disk in the proper disk drives and to boot up the word-processing system without constant teacher supervision. If the computer has a two-disk drive, the student must understand that the program disk always goes in the first disk drive and the data disk always goes in the second disk drive. Teachers have found it helpful to put red stickers on the program disks and the first disk drive and blue stickers on the data disks and the second disk drive so students can remember the correct placement. Also helpful is a wall chart with step-by-step instructions and accompanying drawings.

With a single disk drive, the student must remove the program disk and replace it with the data disk when saving a story. (This is done automatically on a dual disk drive machine.) After the save command is given, there is usually some signal on the monitor that tells the user when to replace the program disk with the data disk and when to put the program disk back in. Because of the need to switch disks back and forth on the single disk drive, third-graders may have more difficulty saving their stories. But with careful instruction and supervision, most should be able to master the process by the end of the year.

As third-graders begin to compose multiparagraph stories, they will need to use the tab key to indent for the beginning of each paragraph. This is easily mastered. It is helpful if the teacher presets the tabs for paragraph indents since this procedure may involve several steps. Third-graders should have little use for other tab settings. Another procedure that can be taught at third grade is centering titles. On most systems centering is simple: the cursor is placed on the line to be centered, the CONTROL key is held down, and the C key is pressed. The computer automatically centers with as many spaces before the words as after. Centering and other similar commands work like on-off switches; if the command is given once, the computer carries it out. To undo the action, the same command is given again.

By the end of the third grade, students should have attained general familiarity with the computer and should be able to write and edit at the word processor with some independence. They should know how to enter a composition into the computer, make revisions, and store it on a diskette. Most will have outgrown the simpler word-processing systems and will be ready to begin using a more powerful system.

Fourth Grade: A Year of Transition

The fourth grade is truly a year of transition. Students have moved from the primary to the intermediate grades. They are approaching the Piagetian stage of formal operations and use more logical thought processes. They are better able to understand the concepts of time and space. In social studies they study cultures vastly different from their own. In science their interests include topics they never encounter directly, such as sharks and distant planets. In writing they start to refer to their compositions as "papers" rather than "stories." Their reading ability has grown to the point that they can read for information, and many become voracious readers on subjects that interest them (Clarke-Stewart, Friedman, and Koch 1985).

The general computer skills of fourth-graders should include booting up educational software without teacher guidance, selecting a teacher-designated lesson from a menu, beginning to write simple computer programs, and understanding how computers are used in the world of work. If keyboarding has been taught in earlier grades, they should be fairly accomplished. If not, there are several excellent programs available for introducing keyboarding skills at this level.

Because of their increasing cognitive skills, longer attention span, and growing verbal facility, fourth-graders are capable of writing simple research reports involving use of the card catalog and reference materials. They need practice in gathering information on a topic and organizing it to present to an audience in writing or orally.

In carrying out revisions and proofreading for errors on their first drafts, students should learn to use the editing marks used by professional editors. Learning to use these marks to indicate copy changes simplifies the revision process and gives students a sense of pride when they can use the same system as editors do. Teachers can find a list of these marks in many college freshman composition texts, dictionaries, or in their language arts textbook.

As their writing improves, many fourth-graders will outgrow the simpler word-processing systems. They will be ready to make the transition to a more powerful package, such as *AppleWorks* (for Apple computers), *SuperScripsit* (for TRS-80 model III and IV computers), or *WordPerfect* (for IBM and Tandy 1000 computers). I recommend introducing these software programs at this time because students are able to compose longer papers and do more extensive revision, which will require a word-processing system that keeps pace with their needs. If teachers carefully introduce the new procedures and allow adequate supervised practice time, students can soon make the transition to a more sophisticated system. Once the more complex system is mastered, students will be able to use it throughout high school, college, and into adulthood. Students who have become "computer experts" are eager to act as peer teachers or troubleshooters, thereby releasing teachers to work individually with students who need more intensive instruction.

As students engage in more complex revisions, such as changing the order of paragraphs or deleting whole sections, a more advanced word-processing system can be of invaluable assistance. With the word processor the student can designate a section of text as a block on which to carry out specific operations. Working on this section will not affect the rest of the composition.

Procedures for carrying out *block commands* can be illustrated by using material printed on large charts or on the chalkboard before implementing it on the computer. To move sentences within a paragraph, the teacher can illustrate by writing the sentences from the paragraph on separate strips of paper and scrambling them. As a sentence is moved, the teacher places an editing mark at its beginning and end and then marks the place in the paragraph where it should be inserted. Executing the procedure on a word processor is done in exactly the same fashion. Using a CONTROL-letter key combination, the user marks the beginning and the end of a sentence or other block of text and designates what the computer is to do with that block. If it is to be moved, the cursor is moved to the place in the document where it is to go, the appropriate command is given, and the computer instantly erases it from the old position and reprints it in the new location.

Another block function useful to students is the *block delete*. This is a quick way to erase a sentence, a paragraph, or even whole pages. Most word-processing systems provide a fail-safe feature; before the delete is carried out, the following question appears on the screen: "You have asked to delete this block. Are you sure? Yes or No." Another safety feature allows the user to recall the deleted text before the delete key is pressed. These features give the user the opportunity to reconsider the decision before permanently erasing the block. Students should be warned to think carefully before deleting large chunks of text because once deleted they are not retrievable. It is good practice for students to develop the habit of making printed copies of successive drafts so that words or ideas are not lost as revision progresses. The block function also can be used to print only a portion of a paper. This comes in handy when students want to see how a section of their paper will look in print, or if they want to use a segment of a composition for some special purpose.

In fourth grade students should learn to instruct the computer to print their papers without teacher assistance. This is done by giving the command for printing (usually CONTROL-P) while in an open document. The student then selects the desired printing options from a list of alternatives displayed on the monitor. These options may in-

The teacher incorporates a lesson on suffixes and prefixes while teaching students how to use the insert command.

clude choosing the number of copies to be printed, deciding whether the printer should pause between pages, and the like. If teachers want to limit the options to be used, they can preset those options and tell students to ignore the others.

It is important to allow students plenty of "play" time for experimenting with each newly introduced command so they get a good feel for what it can do. Teachers can kill two birds with one stone by using language skill worksheets as practice exercises for new word-processing commands. For instance, if students are working on suffixes, the teacher can set up a lesson where the students must use the insert command to add endings to words. Teacher-designed lessons can be quickly copied onto student diskettes using the backup command.

Many systems have *help screens,* which can be displayed at any time without affecting the typed document. These help screens display the various commands so that they can easily be looked up if not memorized. With help screens students do not have to wait for the teacher to get to them when they forget the command for a function.

Teachers have found it helpful to compile individual word-processing manuals for students, which provide a more detailed explanation for the different functions than is available on help screens. Each student's manual might contain guidelines for the care and handling of hardware and software, basic operating procedures for the word-processing system in use, and detailed written and pictorial instructions for those commands the student is currently using. Pages with new commands can be added to manuals as needed.

By the end of the year, most fourth-graders should be fairly capable users of word-processing software. They should be able to carry out simple editing and printing commands without teacher assistance and should have begun to master more complex commands such as blocking. As students undertake more editing and revision of their writing, these commands become very helpful in the various writing stages.

Fifth Grade: Extended Application

Most fifth-graders have the mental capacity to begin to deal with abstract concepts and make logical inferences and predictions. Their understanding of the world about them broadens. They can understand the effects of the past on the present and of the present on the future and may be very interested in history and current events. Their social sphere widens and their interpersonal interaction becomes less self-centered (Clarke-Stewart, Friedman, and Koch 1985).

If fifth-graders have been exposed to a sequential program in earlier grades, they should understand fully how a computer works. They should be familiar with the various input and output devices and be able to identify the sequential flow of data through a computer system. They also should understand the role and function of software and computer languages.

With increasing ability to express themselves, fifth-graders are able to compose themes that may run several pages in length. They can now fully utilize the word processor as a tool to facilitate their writing. This is a good time for them to begin to use a *spelling checker* program if it is available with their word-processing system. This feature is especially useful for students who have difficulty with spelling.

A spelling checker is a diskette containing a list of several thousand words. When put into the disk drive, the computer compares the words the student enters on the keyboard with those on the spelling checker list. If the word is misspelled, the computer highlights the word on the monitor. Then the user must look up the correct spelling and make the necessary changes. If a word entered is not on the spelling checker list (for example, proper names), the computer will highlight the word. In this case the user may take no action or may add the word to the list so that when it appears again it will not be highlighted.

I advocate waiting to introduce spelling checkers until fifth grade because the procedure for using the software is somewhat complicated and younger students may have difficulty managing it. But more important, students should get in the habit of proofreading to detect their own spelling errors before they are allowed to use a computer that does this automatically. If the computer actually corrected the spelling of words, I would not recommend that students be allowed to use spelling checkers. However, since the students must make all corrections themselves, they can improve their spelling by having their mistakes highlighted by the computer.

Although there are different spelling checklist programs, the procedure for using one is fairly standard. The diskette is placed in the disk drive, and the command is given for the function to begin. The user has to designate whether the whole document or only a portion is to be scanned. The computer will then begin rapidly scanning the designated text until it locates the first word in the paper that is not stored in its dictionary. It will highlight this word on the monitor and then display a series of possible changes for dealing with that word. If it is misspelled because of a typo, then the user corrects it. If it is misspelled because the user doesn't know the correct spelling, then the user must look up the spelling in a dictionary.

Students should be aware that spelling checkers cannot detect incorrectly used homophones, such as "to," "two," and "too" or "their" and "there." Neither can it detect errors where a typo on one letter results in a new word that also is on the list, for example "night" and "light." Nuances of the English language still will require much human judgment. Computers are not yet as smart as we are!

By fifth grade many students are doing a fair amount of research. Now they can learn to use the word processor as a note-taking aid. Students first enter the citation for the reference consulted and then type in the information they want underneath. If the research notes are in their own words, students can move those notes from the file and insert them directly into their composition at the appropriate place by using the block copying command. Block copying is done in the same manner as block moving except that the computer does not erase the passage from its original location. The citations also can be easily moved when preparing the bibliography of their paper. Some media centers now have word processors. Student researchers can take their own diskettes to the media center and store their notes for later use when composing in the classroom.

For research papers, fifth-graders should learn the *underlining* command to underline the titles of reference books in their bibliography and to emphasize certain words by underlining. To underline, the user gives the appropriate command, types the text to be underlined, and gives the command to stop underlining (underlining is usually a toggled command). This command can be demonstrated very easily at the board by using a special symbol to mark the beginning and the end of the words to be underlined.

Having the students keep a daily journal provides one of the best ways for developing competent writers: namely, frequent writing practice. Many fifth-graders enjoy keeping a daily journal. Teachers can capitalize on this interest by using journal entries as the source for longer papers. The teacher can ask students to amplify certain journal entries or to connect several entries to form a continuing narrative. Since students are the "expert" on their own life, there is no need to spend time on research; and there is always something to write about.

Students can use individual diskettes to keep their daily journals on the word processor. Privacy is ensured if students store their journals under secret file names. If any entry or series of entries is used as the basis for a paper, the student can copy them into a file to be used for the new document. An outline can be developed using the selected entries, and the students can move rapidly between the outline and its source as they compose their papers.

Fifth-graders will be interested in knowing about the various options for printing, such as changing the number of characters per inch, or using different print wheels for various type styles. These options permit students to vary the format of the printed page as their purpose or audience changes.

Fifth-graders should be able to use the word processor for a variety of purposes and at all stages of writing. By the end of the year they should be so adept at using the various functions of the word processor that the commands can be used almost automatically. They can now begin to develop creative applications in different subject areas.

Sixth Grade: Full Use of the System

The horizons of sixth-graders are rapidly expanding. Although they have not yet fully become abstract thinkers, their cognitive capacity is increasing. They may not be able to apply newly learned concepts in daily life, but this ability will be enhanced with practice. Peers are replacing teachers as the most important influence on students' lives. Strong friendship groups begin to form, and group mores may influence individual attitudes and values (Clarke-Stewart, Friedman, and Koch 1985).

Sixth-graders can begin exploring various computer applications and learn the basics of programming. They also should begin to understand the impact computer technology is having on our society.

The average sixth-grader is able to draft a full-blown research paper as well as a variety of other written compositions. If students have been taught to use a word processor before entering sixth grade, they will be able to move to more sophisticated functions of the system. One of these is the *search* function. This function allows the user to block all or part of the document and specify a particular word or phrase for the computer to locate within the designated block. There are two ways this command can be used. The first is, *search and find*, where the computer finds a specific word in a long paper so that the writer does not have to scan the whole document to locate it. For instance, in a paper about the California gold rush, a student might want to modify a paragraph describing one of the famous lode sites. Using the search and find function, the student can ask the computer to search for "Sutter's Mill," and it will immediately place the cursor on the first time that phrase occurs in the paper. If that is the desired paragraph, the student can cancel the search and begin to rework that section. If the student wants a later mention of Sutter's Mill, the computer can continue searching for that phrase until the right section of the paper is found.

Another search function is *search and replace,* which is used to replace one word or phrase with another. This can speed up the typing task if abbreviations are used when the first draft of the paper is typed. Then when editing later, the computer can replace those abbreviations with the full words or phrases they represent. This function also comes in handy when a word is repeatedly misspelled. All instances of the word can be corrected almost instantaneously. The search and replace function allows the user to make corrections on each separate entry or to have the computer automatically correct all entries for the designated word or phrase.

Writing assignments for sixth-graders should be varied in both content and length. One teacher has his students conduct interviews as the basis for research reports on controversial topics. When possible, he has the students conduct the interviews beside the word processor with prepared questions already stored on diskette. During the interview, the student can record the subject's answers in space allowed under each question and easily insert extra space for answers longer than anticipated. When the research phase is complete, block commands can be used to move responses around and to insert them in the final report at the appropriate spot.

Another project is to have students use the word processor to make up posters or brochures for various purposes. For this kind of assignment, students have to learn how to set up the document as it will appear in print in terms of margins, linespacing, number of characters per inch to be printed, etc. This is called *formatting*. Software packages handle formatting in a variety of ways, so I shall not attempt to provide specific commands here. I do recommend that the software selected provides for *on-screen formatting*. This means the document will appear on the screen exactly as it will look when it is printed. Without on-screen formatting, it can be difficult for students to visualize how the final copy will look when it is printed. Some packages allow the user to make *embedded format commands*. This means that the writer can give commands to the printer in the middle of a document without affecting the rest of that document. A common embedded format command is underlining.

With some software the computer can repeat the same words or phrases on each page of a document, for example, page numbering, chapter titles, or section headings. If a repeated phrase is printed at the top of a page, it is called a *header;* at the bottom of a page, a *footer.* Some students like to put their last names on each page of a document for security purposes. Headers might be used to print the names of individual contributors when a collection of student stories is bound for circulation.

By the end of the sixth grade, if students have had sequential instruction and practice, they will have mastered all of the commands to permit full use of a word-processing system. The word processor will then become a vital tool to use throughout their remaining school years and into adulthood.

Students feel pride at seeing the professional appearance of their work when it is printed by the word processor.

Possible Problems and Some Practical Solutions

Today, the biggest problem facing teachers who wish to use word processors to teach writing is having access to enough computers. The ideal situation would be for each student in the school to have a computer. Because the cost of providing this many computers would be prohibitive for even the most affluent school systems, this ideal is not feasible at the present time.

An alternative that is feasible exists in those schools that have a computer lab. More and more schools now have a computer lab that serves the whole school, but it cannot be scheduled exclusively for teaching writing. However, a teacher can schedule time in the lab each week to work on writing with the whole class. In this setup, a teacher can train students in the basics of word processing and can oversee the stages of the writing process using the computer. Also in a computer lab, related language arts skills can be taught by using software that provides the same on-screen presentation of relevant exercises to each student. With one or two computers in the classroom, students can follow up the work they have done in the lab on an individual basis as scheduling permits.

With a few computers in a classroom, students can use the word processor for all phases of writing. In this setup, the teacher will have to work out a schedule for use of the word processors with each student or groups of students signing up for available time slots. Scheduling, of course, will depend on student interest, regular classroom schedule, and the requirements of different writing assignments. There should be some flexibility in scheduling so that students can use the word processor when other assignments are completed.

Even where there is only one computer in a classroom, the students can do their first draft at their desks and then type it into the word processor for the revision and printing stages. Even with limited computer access, students can overcome the hassles ordinarily involved in writing (Wheeler 1985).

A second problem in teaching writing with word processors is that the students must be trained before they can use the system with facility. With schedules that are already too full, some teachers resent using class time for this training. However, teachers who have begun teaching writing using word processors say that the benefits derived more than justify the time required for training.

Using a word processor does not require computer programming skills; with mastery of the basic commands, students can begin to use the word processor for writing (Hunter 1984; McAllister 1985). Once students understand how the system works, there is no need to bombard them with all possible commands. The more advanced commands can be taught as they are needed. New commands can be practiced using language arts exercises stored on student diskettes. In this way time spent on learning word-processing skills also will be used for learning other language skills. Teacher time also can be saved by using those students who quickly become the class computer "experts" to help slower students (Hunter 1984).

For some teachers a perceived problem is that students first have to be taught proper typing skills before they can use the word processor. But this is not as big a problem as it might at first appear. There are excellent software packages on the market today specifically designed to teach keyboarding to young students. Packages such as *ComputerGarden* for kindergarten and first-grade students and *Rainbow Keyboarding* for second- and third-graders (available from Scholastic, Inc.) have been designed with care, taking developmental patterns of learners into account. These two packages also incorporate subject matter into the learning of keyboarding skills so that these skills are not learned in isolation. Good software also is available to teach keyboarding skills to older students. Because of the highly motivating graphics in this software, students are eager to use their free time to practice keyboarding skills. Both skilled typists and those who hunt and peck say that their speed and accuracy improves on a word processor because they are not so tense about making errors.

If students have access to at least one computer in the classroom, a creative teacher can devise some means of teaching keyboarding skills and use of word-processing software. Teachers who have used word processors to teach writing state that the gains that students make in writing competency is worth the effort.

How to Select Word-Processing Software

Once the decision has been made to use microcomputers to teach writing, selecting the right word-processing package for a particular class is the most important decision a teacher has to make. If unfamiliar with the various software packages, it may be difficult for teachers to know which package is most appropriate for their students. It is preferable to purchase the software from a local computer vendor where a salesperson can demonstrate the different compatible word-processing packages right in the store. (Compatible packages are those that can be used on a particular brand of computer.) The teacher can see how easily the commands are given, determine whether the system has the commands needed for the age level of the students, and evaluate the ease with which the system can be learned. By using a local vendor, the teacher can ask questions before the package is purchased. And if problems arise later, the local vendor is available for consultation. If the software under consideration is not available from a local computer vendor, then the teacher should order it from a company that allows an examination period before billing. If after examination the software is deemed unsuitable, then the teacher can return it with no charge.

Teachers also should consult critical reviews of word-processing software written by practitioners and published in journals devoted to computers in education. There are also articles in these journals written by teachers who have used software packages in their classes in unique and interesting ways. Their suggestions can be very helpful to teachers using word-processing software for the first time. Another way of determining whether a particular word-processing package is appropriate is to discuss it with other teachers who have used it with their students.

When evaluating a word-processing system, teachers should take the time to examine it carefully. Listed below are several points to consider when comparing different systems.

1. Does the software permit the user to edit while in the write mode? The user should be able to make changes in the typed text without having to switch back and forth between the write mode and the edit mode.

2. Does the text displayed on the screen show revisions exactly as they will appear in the printed copy? On-screen formatting greatly facilitates setting up the copy to be printed.

3. Does the software permit both strikeover and insertion of new text? Even those packages designed for very young students should have both features.

4. Is deletion of text easily accomplished with an immediate on-screen display of the revised text? Deleted sections should appear as soon as the delete command is given, even with those packages that have a yankback feature.

5. Does the package permit easy movement of blocks of text both within a single document and between different documents stored on a disk? This feature can greatly facilitate the revision process.

6. Are cursor movement commands easily accomplished with a variety of movements available? The user should be able to move the cursor around in the document easily and quickly. Preference should be given to packages that allow instant movement between pages as well as between lines.

7. Are easily executed embedded format commands, including underlining, boldface, margin adjustments, and variable linespacing available? Even though younger students probably will not be ready to use all these commands, the teacher may need them for preparing student work for display.

8. Does the package allow the user to stop the printer after it has started to print? Often users will see a change that needs to be made after the printer has started; they should be able to stop the printer before it prints the whole document.

9. Does the package allow the user to print small sections of the document? Users should be able to print single pages or small sections when they wish.

10. Are help screens readily available to remind users of available commands? Help screens should be easy to call up and the commands clearly displayed with easy movement among the list.

11. Does the software provide safety features? The delete command should have some fail-safe or yankback feature to prevent loss of material.

12. Is a spelling checker available and is the word list appropriate for students? The vocabularly level of the students is very important

Students work as a group while writing and editing on a word processor.

when selecting a spelling checker. Students in higher grades will quickly fill up a spelling checker list with limited entry space.

13. Does the publisher provide a tutorial tape or diskette? These tutorials can help the new user get a general sense of how the system operates before attempting to master the specific commands (Knapp 1986).

Many people make decisions about which word-processing package to buy based on the ease with which the commands can be given and how quickly the system can be learned. However, trading utility for convenience may be unwise. The more powerful packages may take a bit longer to learn, but their greater usefulness makes the time worthwhile.

Conclusion

Psychologist and computer enthusiast Sherry Turkle predicts that word processors in the schools will cause "an *explosion* of writing" (Rhodes 1986). Word processors can be a powerful catalyst for turning a generation of students into competent writers. And when they are used in classrooms where the process of writing is taught, their power is multiplied manyfold.

In classrooms where students are encouraged to share their ideas and feelings, and where the mechanical procedures required to record and revise those ideas and feelings are made easier, students will want to write. Their writing will become a source of personal pride and accomplishment. Students will begin to write because they enjoy it rather than because they are forced to do so. If we can help elementary students to experience the pleasure of expressing themselves clearly, what a generation of writers we can produce!

References

Britton, J.; Burgess, T.; Martin, N.; McLeod, A.; and Rosen, H. *The Development of Writing Abilities (11-18)*. London: Macmillan Education, 1975.

Clarke-Stewart, A.; Friedman, S.; and Koch, J. *Child Development: A Topical Approach*. New York: John Wiley & Sons, 1985.

Collins, J.L., and Sommers, E.A. *Writing On-Line: Using Computers in the Teaching of Writing*. Upper Montclair, N.J.: Boynton/Cook, 1985.

Emig, J. "Writing as a Mode of Learning." *College Composition and Communication* 28 (1971): 122-28.

Fischer, O.H., and Fischer, C.A. "Electrifying the Composing Process: Electronic Workspaces and the Teaching of Writing." *Journal of Teaching Writing* 4, no. 1 (1985): 113-21.

Hult, C. "A Study of the Effects of Word Processing on the Correctness of Student Writing." Paper presented at the annual meeting of the Conference on College Composition and Communication in Minneapolis, March 1985.

Hunter, L. "Student Responses to Using Computer Text Editing." *Journal of Developmental and Remedial Education* 8, no. 2 (1984): 13-14, 29.

Knapp, L.R. *The Word Processor and the Teacher*. Englewood Cliffs, N.J.: Prentice-Hall, 1986.

Kurth, R.J., and Stromberg, L.J. "Using Word Processing in Composition Instruction." Paper presented at the annual meeting of the American Reading Forum in Sarasota, Fla., December 1984.

McAllister, C. "The Word Processor: A Visual Tool for Writing Teachers." *Journal of Developmental and Remedial Education* 8, no. 3 (1985): 12-15.

Mercer, D.; Correa, V.I.; and Sowell, V. "Teaching Visually Impaired Students Word Processing Competencies: The Use of the Viewscan Textline." *Education of the Visually Handicapped* 17 (1985): 17-29.

Phenix, J., and Hannan, E. "Word Processing in the Grade One Classroom." *Language Arts* 61 (1984): 804-12.

Rhodes, L.A. "On Computers, Personal Styles, and Being Human: A Conversation with Sherry Turkle." *Educational Leadership* (March 1986): 12-16.

Rogers, D. *Life-Span Human Development.* Monterey, Calif.: Brooks/Cole, 1982.

Smith, N.J. "The Word Processing Approach to Language Experience," *The Reading Teacher* 38, no. 6 (1985): 556-59.

Wheeler, F. "Can Word Processing Help the Writing Process?" *Learning* 13, no. 7 (1985): 54, 58, 60, 62.